GREAT BASIN INDIANS

MELISSA MCDANIEL

HEINEMANN LIBRARY
CHICAGO, ILLINOIS

www.heinemannraintree.com
Visit our website to find out more information about Heinemann-Raintree books.

To order:

☎ Phone 888-454-2279

🖳 Visit www.heinemannraintree.com to browse our catalog and order online.

© 2012 Heinemann Library
an imprint of Capstone Global Library, LLC
Chicago, Illinois

Original illustrations © Capstone Global Library, Ltd.
Illustrated by Mapping Specialists, Ltd.
Originated by Capstone Global Library, Ltd.
Printed by China Translation and Printing Company

15 14 13 12 11
10 9 8 7 6 5 4 3 2 1

Library of Congress Cataloging-in-Publication Data
McDaniel, Melissa, 1964-
  Great Basin Indians / Melissa McDaniel.
    p. cm.—(First Nations of North America)
  Includes bibliographical references and index.
  ISBN 978-1-4329-4947-1 (hc)—ISBN 978-1-4329-4958-7
(pb) 1. Indians of North America—Great Basin—Juvenile
literature. 2. Indians of North America—Great Basin—
History—Juvenile literature. I. Title.
  E78.G67M44 2012
  978.004'97—dc22   2010042268

Acknowledgments

The author and publisher are grateful to the following for permission to reproduce copyright material:

Corbis: pp. 4 (© Marilyn Angel Wynn/Nativestock Pictures),13 (© Corbis), 22 (© John K. Hillers); Getty Images: pp. 10 (Jeff Foott), 19 (Marilyn Angel Wynn/Nativestock.com), 23 (Hulton Archive), 38 (Transcendental Graphics); istockphoto: p. 12 (© Lenore Cohen); Library of Congress Prints and Photographs Division: pp. 14, 15, 16, 17, 18, 25, 27, 28, 37; National Park Service: p. 11 (F. Weiss); Nativestock.com: pp. 5 (© Marilyn Angel Wynn), 21 (© Marilyn Angel Wynn), 24 (© Marilyn Angel Wynn), 26 (© Marilyn Angel Wynn), 29 (© Marilyn Angel Wynn), 31 (© Marilyn Angel Wynn), 32 (© Marilyn Angel Wynn), 33 (© Marilyn Angel Wynn), 39 (© Marilyn Angel Wynn), 41 (© Marilyn Angel Wynn); Shutterstock: p. 35 (© 7716430100); The Granger Collection, NYC: pp. 20, 34.

Cover photograph of a Buffalo hunt illustration on elk skin by the Shoshone Katsikodi School reproduced with permission from The Bridgeman Art Library International (The Stapleton Collection).

We would like to thank Dr. Scott Stevens for his invaluable help in the preparation of this book.

Every effort has been made to contact copyright holders of any material reproduced in this book. Any omissions will be rectified in subsequent printings if notice is given to the publisher.

Contents

Some words are shown in bold **like this**. You can find out what they mean by looking in the glossary.

Who Were the First People in North America?

How long would you survive in a **desolate** land with little rain, few trees, fewer rivers, and scarce animals? What would you eat? Early Great Basin Indians learned to rely on what nature could provide. They found food from more than 100 different wild plants. They built homes from limited supplies. The early Great Basin Indians not only survived. They also developed a rich **culture** in one of the most unwelcoming lands on Earth.

Today, American Indians still live in the Great Basin and other parts of North America. They are the **descendants** of the first people to arrive on the continent. Many modern American Indians carry on the traditions and customs of their **ancestors**. This book will discuss the Indians who live in the part of North America called the Great Basin.

▲ Today, about 2.5 million American Indians live in the United States. They belong to hundreds of different **nations**.

Why are they called American Indians?

Different terms are used to describe American Indians. Italian explorer Christopher Columbus sailed across the Atlantic Ocean to North America in 1492. Thinking he was in the Indies, a region of Asia, he called the people he encountered Indians.

People from the Asian country of India are also called Indians. To cut down on the confusion, the descendants of the first people in North America are sometimes called American Indians.

They are also often called Native Americans, because their cultures arose in North America. Different people prefer different terms. But many American Indians prefer to be called by the name of their unique group, called a nation or **tribe**—for example, Shoshone.

▼ Early Great Basin Indians were very skilled hunters.

The first American Indians

People probably first arrived in North America more than 12,000 years ago. This was during the last major ice age, when much of the planet's water was frozen into ice. Because of this, sea levels were lower. Today, ocean water separates Alaska from Russia. But scientists believe that back then, a wide stretch of dry land connected the two regions. People from Asia walked across this land to enter a different continent.

These first North Americans were **nomadic** hunters, traveling from place to place in search of animals to hunt, called **game**. Over the course of several thousand years, these people spread all across the continent.

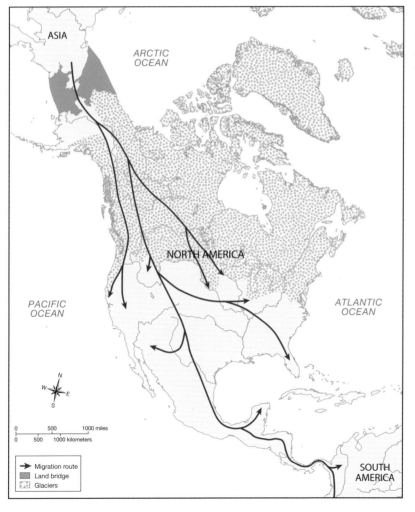

◄ This map shows some of the routes early peoples took as they spread across North America.

◄ This map shows the 10 American Indian culture areas of North America.

Culture areas

Early peoples settled in different parts of North America. Those who lived in the same regions often shared similar ways of life. This allows people who study American Indian societies to group them into **culture areas**.

One of these culture areas is the Great Basin. The Great Basin is in what is now the western United States. It lies between the Rocky Mountains to the east and the Sierra Nevada to the west. The Great Basin covers almost all of present-day Nevada and Utah, along with western Colorado and Wyoming, southern Idaho, southeastern Oregon, and slivers of California, Arizona, and New Mexico. The early peoples of North America first began arriving in the Great Basin about 10,000 years ago.

American Indian nations

Even within the same culture area, Indian groups developed customs and ways of life that were different from each other. Ever since, each group has had its own culture. They each have their own religion, their own language, and their own ways of doing things.

These American Indian groups are called nations, or tribes. Each culture area includes many different nations of peoples. The major American Indian nations in the Great Basin include:

Ute

The Ute people traditionally lived in small groups, or **bands**, and moved frequently in search of food. They first acquired horses in the 1600s. After this, Utes became great traders and became notable raiders.

Paiute

The traditional lands of the Paiute people cover much of the Great Basin. The Paiutes are divided into two groups—the Northern Paiutes and the Southern Paiutes. In the past, Paiutes moved often to hunt and gather the food they needed to survive.

Bannock

The Bannock people are closely related to the Northern Paiutes. Bannocks began using horses in the 1700s, which allowed them to travel over a wide area in search of food.

Shoshone

The Shoshone people are divided into three large groups: Western, Northern, and Eastern. In the past, Western Shoshones survived by gathering plants. Northern Shoshones fished, hunted big game, and dug roots. After getting horses in the 1700s, Eastern Shoshones hunted antelope and bison. Shoshones are known for their detailed beadwork.

Washoe

The Washoe people live in the mountains on the border between California and Nevada. Lake Tahoe, a large lake high in the mountains, is the center of their spiritual world. In the past, Washoes lived by hunting, fishing, and gathering nuts. Their baskets are highly prized.

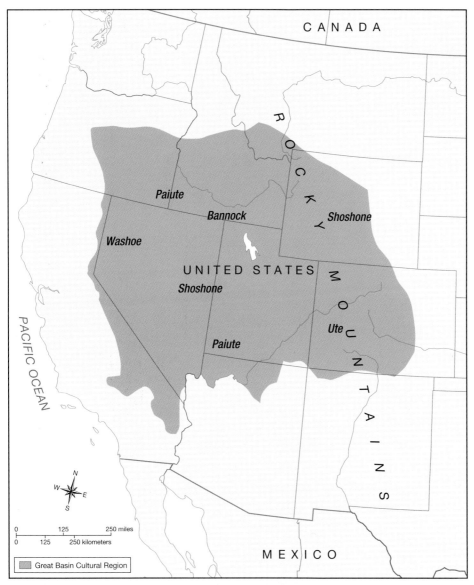

▲ This map shows some of the traditional **tribal** homelands of the Great Basin.

Who Were the First People in the Great Basin?

People first arrived in the Great Basin more than 10,000 years ago. These early hunters, now called **Paleo-Indians**, wandered from place to place in search of **game**. They hunted large creatures such as mammoths—relatives of the elephant—and giant ground sloths.

By 6,000 years ago, these large animals had died out. People were instead hunting deer and rabbits. Food from plants also became more important, and people began grinding seeds into flour. This is known as the Desert **Archaic culture**.

In about 400 CE, a new culture emerged in the Great Basin. The Fremont people hunted and gathered plants, but they also grew corn, beans, and squash.

▶ The Fremont people made more than 10,000 pictures on the walls of Nine Mile Canyon, in eastern Utah.

They built stone storage buildings for their crops. Traces of the Fremont culture are visible in the vibrant pictures they painted on cliff walls.

Other people began moving into the Great Basin from present-day southern California about 1,000 years ago. They may have merged with the Fremont people or pushed them out. Either way, they quickly adapted to the Great Basin. They became the Ute, Paiute, and Shoshone **nations**.

ART AND CULTURE

Danger Cave

The early Great Basin Indians took shelter in a cave known as Danger Cave, in the **barren** high desert of western Utah. In the 1940s, an **archaeologist** named Jesse Jennings began studying the cave. He dug down into the cave floor, finding layer after layer of **artifacts**—at least 37 layers in all. He found tools, knives, nets, fabric, and more. The oldest items dated back more than 10,000 years. By studying the artifacts, Jennings shed light on the culture of the early Utahans.

▲ Danger Cave was declared a national landmark by the U.S. government in 1961. This honor is given only to places of special historic significance.

What Is Land in the Great Basin Like?

The Great Basin is a harsh and unforgiving land. It consists of a series of broad valleys separated by mountain ranges. The valleys are **barren** (bare), while the mountain peaks are high and grand.

The Great Basin is one of the most difficult places to live in North America. Much of it is desert, getting just 6 to 12 inches (15 to 30 centimeters) of rain each year. Streams are few and far between. And many of the lakes are salty, so their water cannot be used for drinking or watering crops.

▲ The Great Basin is a high desert. Some of the valleys are 6,000 feet (1,800 meters) above sea level.

In the winter, the valley temperatures often drop below freezing. In the summer, it is brutally hot. The mountains are cooler in the summer, but heavy snow blankets them in the winter.

In the valleys, there are no trees to provide welcoming shade. For mile after mile, there is nothing but rocky ground supporting low bushes. In this dry and **desolate** landscape, large animals are rare, though some live in the pine forests on mountain slopes.

Surviving in the Great Basin

Few plants and animals survive in the Great Basin. So, in the past, American Indians had to have detailed knowledge of the land to survive. They knew where and when certain plants produced fruit or seeds. They moved frequently to gather different plant products.

Water was a precious resource for American Indians living a traditional life in the Great Basin. Because the land is so dry, Indians carried their own supply of water.

▼ A Southern Paiute women carries water in a pottery jug. Dry conditions required Great Basin Indians to carry their own water supply.

How Were Early Great Basin Communities Organized?

In the Great Basin, early peoples traditionally lived in small groups of just one or two families. These groups might have just 20 people in them. Food was too scarce for large groups of people to live together.

Each small group had a leader chosen by the members of the community. People selected leaders who had broad knowledge and good judgment. Paiutes, for example, elected leaders who were skilled at settling disputes.

▲ Great Basin Indians, such as these Utes, lived in small groups to help conserve resources such as food.

The leader's most important job was to make sure people had enough food. He kept track of which plants and animals were available. He knew when and where the group should move. The leader was also responsible for leading the group in battle.

If the leader was not successful at these tasks, people would often leave and join a different group. Sometimes they would start their own group. The membership of groups changed frequently.

▶ Great Basin Indians relied on the knowledge of their elders. This Paiute elder was photographed in 1924 by the famous photographer Edward Curtis.

Languages of the Great Basin

Throughout their history, Great Basin Indians have spoken a variety of languages. Paiutes, Utes, and Shoshones all speak Shoshonean languages. These languages are part of the Uto-Aztecan language group. They are related to the language spoken by the Aztecs, a powerful civilization that once dominated central Mexico. Although Paiutes, Utes, and Shoshones speak related languages, their languages are different enough that they cannot understand each other.

The language of the Washoe people is different from that of other Great Basin peoples. It is distantly related to languages spoken by American Indians of California.

What Were Early Great Basin Families Like?

In the **culture** of early Great Basin Indians, grandparents, parents, and children traditionally lived together. It was also common for the families of two brothers to live together. A newly married couple would sometimes live near the bride's parents, and sometimes near the groom's parents.

Great Basin Indians were traditionally warm and welcoming to cousins, aunts, uncles, and other relatives. This friendliness made it easy for people to join other groups that included distant relatives.

◄ In the early Great Basin, many different family members helped take care of the children.

◄ Wearing the baby allowed early Great Basin Indian mothers to keep their babies close and protected while they continued with their daily activities.

Caring for children

In early Great Basin cultures, parents kept their babies in a **cradleboard**—a tradition that some American Indians continue to this day. A cradleboard consists of a wood or basketry framework with a large pouch attached. The baby fits safely and snugly inside the pouch. A mother can wear a cradleboard on her back. This allows her to carry the baby and still have her hands free. A cradleboard can also be hung from a horse or propped up against a tree. In early Great Basin cultures, babies traditionally spent most of the first year of their lives in cradleboards.

Great Basin parents spent most of their time gathering food. Because they were so busy, grandparents often took care of the children. They taught the children how to behave properly and how to survive in the harsh land.

Parents and grandparents taught children important life skills at a young age. Most of these skills centered on finding food. Women taught girls to prepare food. Boys learned to hunt. Utes and Shoshones also taught boys to ride horses.

How Did Early Peoples Survive in the Great Basin?

Traditionally, life was difficult for early peoples of the Great Basin. Food was scarce in this land of scorching heat, brutal cold, **arid** (very dry) land, and salty lakes.

Fall was the one time of year when food was sometimes more plentiful. During the fall, small groups that spent most of the year on their own gathered together for a rabbit hunt or nut harvest. These large gatherings provided essential food, but they also gave people the chance to see old friends. It was a time for prayers and dances.

▶ Each spring, early Great Basin Indians spent time fishing and hunting plants before the intense summer heat arrived.

When winter came and snow blanketed the ground, people retreated to caves or huts. During the long winter, there were few plants to gather, and **game** was rare. People lived on dried food such as fish, rabbits, and berries that they had preserved earlier in the year. Because they seldom searched for food in the winter, Great Basin Indians passed the time telling stories.

Spring arrives

When ducks and geese began flying overhead, people in the Great Basin knew spring was just around the corner. They emerged from their shelters to hunt birds and gather the first tender plant shoots they could find. As the days grew warmer, people found more plants to eat. Spring was also a time for fishing.

Summer was a difficult time in the Great Basin. Plants shriveled in the heat. During summer, some Indians moved higher in the mountains, where it was cooler and berries and other plant foods ripened later in the year.

▲ This Shoshone Bannock man wears a buffalo robe to stay warm during a winter snowstorm.

▲ In the Great Basin, children learned life skills at a young age.

A DAY IN THE LIFE OF AN EARLY PAIUTE CHILD

If you were a Paiute child, one of the best times of year would be the piñon harvest. In the early morning, you head into the piñon forest with all your friends and relatives. Your father carries a long stick. He reaches it high into tree branches and knocks the pinecones to the ground. You climb trees and drop the cones, sending them down to the ground. Your sister fills baskets with the cones and carries them back to camp. Your mother removes the small nuts from the cones and roasts the nuts in a basket filled with hot coals. She will grind the roasted nuts into a paste. The piñon nuts make a delicious soup.

At the end of the long day, a fire glows in the darkness. An old man scatters a few nuts on the ground. He and others dance, sing, and pray, giving thanks for what the Earth has given them.

Early Great Basin gatherers

Food was scarce during the time of the early Great Basin Indians. People had to travel over a wide area to find enough food for themselves and their families.

Wild plants provided most of their main food. They ate roots, seeds, berries, leaves, and grasses. The bulbs of the **camas** lily were a staple for people in the northern Great Basin. The bulbs look like onions, but they are sweet. In the fall, people gathered at groves of **piñon** pine trees to harvest the pine nuts.

▲ Edible berries, roots and bulbs such as choke cherries, bitterroots, camas, and khouse were a major source of food.

Early Great Basin hunters

In much of the Great Basin, there were few large animals. Hunters set their sights on smaller animals, such as rabbits.

A rabbit hunt involved many people working together. People spread out with large nets, sometimes about 1 mile (1.5 kilometers) long. Other people would run, stamp, and yell, to frighten the hiding rabbits. As the rabbits scurried from the bushes, people would chase them into the nets. One hunt could snare hundreds of rabbits.

◄ Early Great Basin Indians used bows and arrows to hunt whatever antelope and deer they could find.

Great Basin Indians also captured lizards and insects to roast and eat. In the **barren** Great Basin, insects like grasshoppers or ants provided nourishment.

Large game

Sometimes, the antelope population of the Great Basin was so large that Great Basin Indians could hold group hunts. Shoshones lived on the forested mountain slopes on the edge of the Great Basin. There, they used bows and arrows to hunt deer, antelope, and mountain sheep.

In the 1700s, Shoshones and Utes got horses from southern relatives. The Spanish had brought horses to North America. Horses helped Great Basin Indians hunt large game. On horseback, hunters traveled faster and farther.

In the spring, Great Basin Indians who lived near water fished for salmon, trout, and remora. They used nets, wicker baskets, or spears to catch the fish.

▲ The introduction of horses helped Great Basin Indians hunt large game more effectively.

What Were Early Great Basin Indian Houses Like?

In the past, Great Basin Indians moved around a great deal in their search for food. Because of this, their houses needed to be easy to build.

For much of the year, the weather was warm, so they did not need elaborate shelters. Often they just needed something that would protect them from the Sun's rays. They typically built a simple wooden framework that they covered with small branches and grasses. In the winter, people built strong domed huts made of willow branches. They covered these huts with mats of woven grass.

▲ Washoe winter houses were windproof and rainproof.

◄ Shoshones made tipis out of bison skins.

More trees grew in the lands of the Washoe people. This allowed them to build larger winter homes. They built these homes partly underground. They began by digging down several feet into the earth. They then put large logs upright in the ground and tied them together. Next, they tied on smaller logs and branches. They covered this sturdy framework first with brush and grass and then with dirt. Washoes moved around for much of the year, living in small huts, but they then returned to these houses winter after winter. They were the only permanent houses built by Great Basin Indians.

Tipis

Because Shoshones hunted larger **game**, they could use animal skins when building their shelters. Shoshones lived in cone-shaped tents called **tipis**. Long poles made the framework of a tipi. Animal skins covered the poles, leaving only a flap for a door and a hole at the top for smoke to escape. Tipis could be built and taken down quickly. Shoshones could pack up their village in an hour.

What Clothing Did Early Great Basin Indians Wear?

Today, Great Basin Indians dress the same as other Americans. In the Great Basin, this often means jeans and T-shirts. In the past, however, their clothes were very different.

Most Shoshone clothing was made from deerskin. Shoshone women wore long deerskin dresses. Men wore leggings and **breechcloths**, which were garments worn between the legs and tucked over a belt. When the weather grew cool, Shoshone men added shirts to their outfits. Shoshones often decorated their dresses and shirts with beads or porcupine quills. Both men and women wore shoes called **moccasins**.

Because most other Great Basin Indians did not frequently hunt large **game**, they could not make clothes from deerskin. They also did not have cotton or wool to use to make clothing or blankets.

▶ Shoshone clothing was often decorated with fancy beadwork.

Summer clothing

In the summer, many Great Basin Indians traditionally wore very few clothes. The weather was scorching, so they did not need any. Sometimes women wore small skirts made of bark or woven grass. Men might wear breechcloths. Some people wore moccasins. Others wore sandals made from reeds. Children typically wore nothing at all.

Winter clothing

Only in the winter did the Great Basin Indians wear more clothing. Although some wore clothing made from deer or bison, many wore rabbit skins. They used the rabbit skins to make capes. Rather than sewing the skins together to make the cape, they cut the rabbit skins into long strips. They twisted each strip fur-side out and then wove the twisted strips together. The result was an extremely warm cape that was furry on both the inside and the outside.

▲ Traditional rabbit-skin capes were lightweight but warm.

What Kind of Objects Do Great Basin Indians Make?

In the past, Great Basin Indians put most of their energy into finding food, so they made objects that were useful. Baskets were the most common craft. They made baskets to carry goods and to store foods. They made basketry **cradleboards**, hats, bowls, and traps.

Washoes and Paiutes also made pottery. They made cooking and storage pots, spoons, water jars, and more.

Washoe baskets

In the late 1800s, a Washoe woman named Datsolalee, also known as Louisa Keyser, created intricate baskets in elegant shapes. Her baskets were so detailed that they sometimes took a year to complete. Today, Washoe basketry is highly prized. Washoes use willow, ferns, reeds, sagebrush, and other plants to weave their baskets.

◄ Washoes made baskets that were light, durable, and beautiful. This is a tradition that continues to this day.

▲ Some Shoshone paintings are on elk skin, while others are on buffalo hide.

Shoshone crafts

The Shoshone Indians are famed for their beadwork. In earlier times, beads were often made from seeds or animal teeth and bones. Today, some are made from pottery, but most are made from cut glass. Some Shoshone beadwork has strong geometric designs, featuring triangle and zigzag patterns. Flower patterns are also common. Shoshone beadwork adorns all kinds of items, from dresses to **moccasins**, and from belts to horse harnesses. It is a skill that is handed down through families, typically from mother to child.

Shoshones also have a history of painting on animal skins. These paintings often depict dances or tell the story of an important event like a successful hunt. Traditionally, the painted skin would be part of a **tipi** or a robe.

What Are the Religious Beliefs of Great Basin Indians?

Each American Indian group has its own religion. But these many religions have some things in common. In all of these religions, powerful spirits are believed to affect human life. Many of these spirits are associated with animals. In the Great Basin, Coyote and Wolf are important. Wolf is often considered the father of the people. Coyote is a trickster who likes to make mischief.

STORIES AND LEGENDS

"The Shake of a Rattle"

Great Basin Indians tell stories to explain their world. This Paiute tale explains their beliefs about how the world was created.

The world was once covered with water. Only one mountain peak rose above the lapping waves. Fish-Eater and Hawk lived on this mountain with all the people. One day, Fish-Eater and Hawk were singing, and Hawk was shaking a rattle. Suddenly, dirt began falling out of the rattle. All night long, Fish-Eater and Hawk sang and shook the rattle. Dirt kept falling into the water below, where it formed land. Finally, enough dirt fell into the water that the water withdrew from around the mountain peak. Hawk then shook the rattle some more and built up the Sierra Nevada Mountains to hold the ocean back.

Finally, Fish-Eater and Hawk were done making Earth. Hawk said, "Well, we have finished. Here is a rabbit to eat. I will live on rabbits for the rest of my life." The people then came down from the mountain and spread out over the land.

Spirits are sometimes said to bring good fortune, like a good harvest. They can also bring misfortune, like illnesses. In the Great Basin, people traditionally held **ceremonies** after successful hunts and **piñon** harvests to give thanks to the spirits.

▲ Shoshones drum and sing traditional songs during religious ceremonies.

▲ A Shoshone spiritual leader and medicine man holds an eagle staff wrapped with wild sage during a ground blessing ceremony in Idaho.

Religious leaders

In Great Basin religions, spirits are believed to appear in dreams, where they grant the dreamer a power. This power might give the person special skills or success.

The spirits are sometimes said to call a particular person to become a religious leader. A person called to be a religious leader learns skills from older religious leaders. Religious leaders can be either men or women. Religious leaders are said to be able to communicate with the spirits, cure illnesses, and sometimes tell the future.

Religious leaders lead **rituals** and ceremonies. Some religious leaders focus on maintaining good weather or preventing bad events from happening. Others focus on making the sick healthy again. To help the sick, religious leaders lead ceremonies that sometimes last several days. Family members often gather for these healing ceremonies.

The Native American Church

In the 1900s, many Great Basin Indians joined the Native American Church. This church mixes traditional American Indian religions with aspects of Christianity. The church stresses ethical behavior, meaning a sense of right and wrong, as well as brotherly love.

Members of the Native American Church sometimes hold ceremonies that last all night. In these ceremonies, people eat parts of the **peyote** cactus. Eating peyote gives a person visions. During these visions, the person is believed to be able to communicate with god or spirit beings. The person also gains guidance and strength.

▲ A church on a Shoshone **reservation** in Wyoming is decorated with traditional Native American designs.

Who Else Came to the Great Basin?

When Spanish explorers first arrived in the Americas in 1492, Spain was the most powerful country on Earth. The Spanish were soon **plundering** the Americas for riches. In 1598 they founded settlements in present-day New Mexico. But it was more than 100 years before they began exploring the **desolate** regions farther north. By the late 1700s, a few Spaniards were trading with Utes, but the Great Basin Indians mostly remained isolated.

Meanwhile, far to the east, the United States was being born in the 1700s. The country began as 13 states lining the East Coast, but it expanded quickly.

▲ Some Mountain Men, such as Jedidiah Smith, were Americans. Others, like Étienne Provost, were French-Canadian.

Mountain Men

Beginning in the 1820s, American and Canadian trappers, traders, and explorers known as Mountain Men crisscrossed the Great Basin. They traveled through the Rocky Mountains and the Great Basin, trapping beavers and other fur-bearing animals. American Indians traded furs with the Mountain Men in exchange for knives and other goods. Little did the Indians know that the trickle of newcomers would soon become a flood.

BIOGRAPHY

Sacagawea: Guide to Lewis and Clark

In the winter of 1804-05, a Northern Shoshone woman named Sacagawea (c. 1788-1812) met U.S. explorers Meriwether Lewis and William Clark, in what is now North Dakota. President Thomas Jefferson had sent Lewis and Clark to explore the West. Lewis and Clark hired Sacagawea as an **interpreter**. On the trail, she helped them communicate with Shoshones and trade for the horses they needed. She helped guide them through the rugged land and taught them about many edible plants.

▲ Sacagawea's son, Jean Baptiste Charbonneau, accompanied his mother on the Lewis and Clark **expedition**.

How Did Life Change for the Great Basin Indians?

In the 1800s, Americans in the East set their sights on the **fertile** valleys of the West Coast of North America. In 1843 the first wagon train of settlers snaked its way across Shoshone land on a pathway that would become the Oregon Trail. In the next 25 years, half a million settlers would make the journey west. This steady flow of settlers used up precious water, and the settlers' animals trampled some plants the Indians needed to survive.

▼ This map shows some of the trails used by migrating non-Indians as they traveled westward.

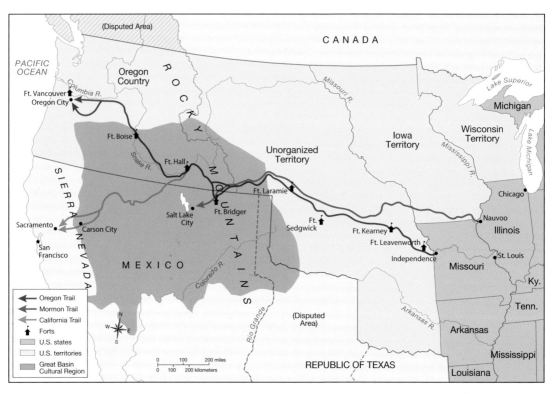

◀ The mining town of Gold Hill, Nevada is shown here about 1872. At its peak, the town had approximately 8,000 residents. In 2005 the population was around 191.

The Mormon Trail

In 1847 members of the Church of Jesus Christ of the Latter-Day Saints, commonly called Mormons, began heading west to Utah. They wanted to start their own community far away from other people, so they could practice their religion in peace. They established Salt Lake City and other towns near Shoshone lands. They soon pushed farther south, founding towns in Paiute and Ute territory. This forced Indians from their traditional hunting and gathering areas.

Gold rush

In 1849 the California Gold Rush began. Hopeful U.S. miners poured across Paiute land to the gold fields. In 1859 gold and silver were discovered in Nevada, and miners charged into Washoe territory. The newcomers chopped down important **piñon** groves. They fished Washoe waters and hunted their **game**.

Hard times

Throughout the Great Basin, American Indians could no longer find enough food. They sometimes raided the newcomers' settlements so they would not starve. The U.S. government responded brutally. In 1863 the U.S. Army attacked a Shoshone camp on the Bear River in present-day southern Idaho. The soldiers killed every Shoshone they could find—more than 350 men, women, and children.

Reservations

In 1851 the U.S. government began establishing **reservations**, land set aside for American Indian use only. Indians were forced to move from the land they had lived on for thousands of years. They were required to live, hunt, and gather solely on the reservations. But in the **arid** Great Basin, the reservation land did not provide enough food. Great Basin Indians struggled to survive.

BIOGRAPHY

Sarah Winnemucca: Speaking Out

Sarah Winnemucca experienced the upheaval of miners overrunning Paiute land, yet she worked for peace. Winnemucca served as an **interpreter** for the U.S. Army. Starting in 1879, she traveled to California and the East Coast, giving speeches about reservation life. She told how the government officials in charge of reservations were dishonest and treated Indians badly. She talked about how the Paiutes were starving. Winnemucca did much to shed light on the **plight** of Great Basin Indians. There is a statue in her honor in Washington, D.C.

▲ Winnemucca was the first American Indian woman to publish in the English language.

▲ While performing the Ghost Dance, some dancers fell into trances.

Indians fought against being forced to live on reservations. In 1865 Utes, Paiutes, and others began fighting the Black Hawk War to try to prevent the expansion of Mormon settlements. They were not successful.

The Ghost Dance

In 1889 a Paiute named Wovoka became the leader of the Ghost Dance Movement. Ghost Dancers believed that if Indians cooperated with each other and performed the Ghost Dance, then their ancestors and game would return and the old Indian world would be restored. Non-Indian people would vanish from the land.

The Ghost Dance Movement spread throughout the western United States. Although the movement was peaceful, it frightened some non-Indians. The U.S. Army tried to stop the Ghost Dance, but the movement and its message endured in the Great Basin.

What Is Life Like Today for the Great Basin Indians?

The Great Basin is still home to many American Indians. About 31,000 Indians live in Nevada, and more than 31,000 live in Utah. Some live on **reservations**, while many others live off the reservations, in big cities, small towns, and the countryside. They are doctors, businesspeople, miners, teachers, factory workers, and more.

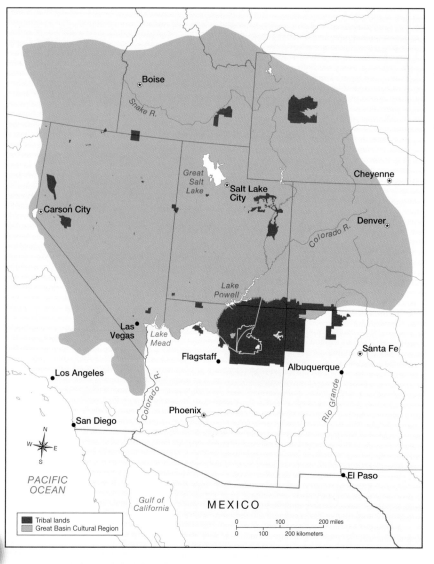

◄ This map shows the location of reservations in the Great Basin cultural region.

Boise

Snake R.

Great
Salt
Lake

Salt Lake
City

Cheyenne

Carson City

Colorado R.

Denver

Lake
Powell

Las
Vegas

Lake
Mead

Santa Fe

Flagstaff

Albuquerque

Los Angeles

Colorado R.

Phoenix

Rio Grande

San Diego

N
W   E
S

El Paso

PACIFIC
OCEAN

Gulf of
California

MEXICO

Tribal lands
Great Basin Cultural Region

0   100   200 miles
0   100   200 kilometers

◄ A Shoshone woman teaches her granddaughter about traditional beadwork.

Reservations today

Today, there are more than two dozen Indian reservations in the Great Basin. Most are small. But the Uintah and Ouray Reservation, a Ute reservation in Utah, is the second-largest reservation in the United States.

Since 1934 American Indians have had the right to elect their own **tribal** council and govern their reservations themselves. The tribal governments work to promote business, tourism, and ranching on the reservations.

Many reservations run their own schools. At these schools, children study standard school subjects along with their traditional **culture** and language. In the Great Basin, few American Indians speak their traditional language, so the schools are playing an important role in helping preserve the culture.

Preserving culture

Great Basin Indians are also preserving their culture in other ways. Some are working to protect their traditional **sacred** sites. Others are working to conserve the fragile **environment** of the Great Basin. And many Great Basin Indians attend traditional celebrations and **ceremonies**. In the dusty deserts and cool **piñon** groves, they take part in some of the same **rituals** and dances that their **ancestors** performed hundreds of years before.

41

Timeline

about 10,000 BCE   The first people arrive in North America.

4000 BCE   The Desert **Archaic culture** thrives.

about 400 CE   The Fremont culture arises.

about 1000   The **ancestors** of the Utes, Paiutes, and Shoshones move into the Great Basin.

1600s   Utes and Spaniards begin trading.

late 1700s   The Spanish enter the Great Basin.

1804–06   Sacagawea serves as an **interpreter** and guide for Meriwether Lewis and William Clark.

1820s   Mountain Men begin trading with Great Basin Indians.

1841   The first organized party sets out on the pathway that becomes the Oregon Trail.

1847   Mormons begin arriving in Utah.

1849   The California Gold Rush begins, and miners streams across Paiute lands.

1851   The United States Congress passed the Indian Appropriations Act which authorized the creation of Indian **reservations** in modern day Oklahoma.

1859   The Comstock Lode, the first major U.S. discovery of gold and silver, is discovered in Washoe territory.

1863   The U.S. Army attacks a Shoshone camp in Bear River, Idaho, killing more than 350 men, women, and children.

1865   The Black Hawk War (in Utah) begins.

1879   Sarah Winnemucca starts giving speeches about the **plight** of the Paiutes. She will give hundreds of lectures throughout the 1880s.

1889   A Paiute named Wovoka begins leading the Ghost Dance movement.

1934   The U.S. Congress passes the Indian Reorganization Act to keep reservation lands under **tribal** ownership and give the **nations** more power to govern the reservations.

1968   The American Indian Movement (AIM) organizes protests against the unfair treatment of American Indians and calls on the government to keep its promises to the people.

1990   Congress passes the Native American Language Act, "to preserve, protect, and promote the rights and freedoms of all native Americans to use, practice and develop Native American Languages."

1990   President George H. W. Bush proclaims the first National American Indian Heritage Month. President Clinton affirms this special designation in November 1996.

2004   The National Museum of the American Indian is established on the National Mall in Washington, D.C.

2010   More than 62,000 American Indians live in Nevada and Utah.

Glossary

ancestor family member from the distant past

archaeologist scientist who studies bones and items left behind by ancient people to learn about the past

archaic typical of an earlier time

arid very dry

artifact object made by humans from an earlier time

band Indian family group that lived together

barren producing few plants

breechcloth garment worn between the legs and tucked over a belt

camas plant in the lily family with an edible bulb

ceremony religious event or observance

cradleboard wooden frame used to carry a baby

culture shared ways of life and beliefs of a group of people

culture area region of North America in which Indians traditionally had a similar way of life

descendant offspring of an earlier group

desolate lacking signs of life

environment natural surroundings

expedition trip for the purpose of exploration

fertile able to produce plentiful crops

game wild animals hunted for food

interpreter person who translates for people speaking different languages

moccasin soft shoe made of animal skin

nation group of people with its own territory

nomadic moving from place to place without a fixed home

Paleo-Indians first people to enter and live in the Americas

peyote part of a cactus that will produce visions when eaten

piñon small pine tree that produces edible seeds

plight bad condition

plunder steal by force

reservation area of land in the United States put aside for the use of American Indians

ritual formal acts or series of acts performed according to a set of rules, often having to do with religion

sacred holy

tipi portable, tent-like dwelling made with wooden poles and animal skins

tribal belonging to or relating to a tribe

tribe group of American Indians who share a culture

Find Out More

Books

Dennis, Yvonne Wakim, and Arlene Hirschfelder. *A Kid's Guide to Native American History: More Than 50 Activities.* Chicago: Chicago Review, 2010.

Ditchfield, Christin. *The Shoshone.* New York: Franklin Watts, 2005.

Shull, Jodie A. *Voice of the Paiutes: A Story about Sarah Winnemucca.* Minneapolis: Millbrook, 2007.

Sonneborn, Liz. *The Mormon Trail.* New York: Franklin Watts, 2005.

Websites

Native Americans in Early Nevada
http://nevada-history.org/indians.html
Learn more about the history of Native Americans in Nevada.

Native Americans in Utah
http://historytogo.utah.gov/utah_chapters/american_indians/
nativeamericansinutah.html
Learn more about the history of Native Americans in Utah.

New Perspectives on the West: Jack Wilson
www.pbs.org/weta/thewest/people/s_z/wovoka.htm
Read about the Paiute mystic who spread the Ghost Dance among many tribes across the American West.

Women of the Hall: Sarah Winnemucca
www.greatwomen.org/women.php?action=viewone&id=172
Read Sarah Winnemucca's biography page at the National Women's Hall of Fame website.

DVDs

The Spirit of Sacagawea. Directed by Beverly Penninger and Alyson Young. Charlotte, N.C.: Naka Productions, 2006.

The West. Directed by Ken Burns. Alexandria, Va.: PBS Paramount, 2004.

Places to visit

Great Basin National Park
100 Great Basin National Park
Baker, NV
www.nps.gov/grba/

Nine Mile Canyon
Price, Utah
www.utah.com/playgrounds/nine_mile.htm

Pyramid Lake Paiute Tribe Museum and Visitor Center
Nixon, NV
http://plpt.nsn.us/museum/index.html

National Museum of the American Indian
Fourth Street and Independence Avenue, SW
Washington, D.C.
www.nmai.si.edu

Further research

What parts of the Great Basin lifestyle did you find the most interesting? How does life for native peoples in the Great Basin compare to the way native peoples live today in other regions? How did the peoples who first lived in your area contribute to life today? To learn more about the Great Basin or other culture areas, visit one of the suggested places on these pages or head to your local library for more information.

Index